W9-ANI-796

WORLD BOOK'S
LIBRARY OF NATURAL DISASTERS

PANDEMICS

WORLD
BOOK

a Scott Fetzer company
Chicago
www.worldbookonline.com

World Book, Inc.
233 N. Michigan Avenue
Chicago, IL 60601
U.S.A.

614.4
World

For information about other World Book publications, visit our Web site at **http://www.worldbookonline.com** or call **1-800-WORLDBK (967-5325).**

For information about sales to schools and libraries, call **1-800-975-3250 (United States); 1-800-837-5365 (Canada).**

2nd edition

The Library of Congress has cataloged an earlier edition of this title as follows:

Pandemics.

    p. cm. -- (World Book's library of natural disasters)
    Summary: "A discussion of major types of natural disasters, including descriptions of some of the most destructive; explanations of these phenomena, what causes them, and where they occur; and information about how to prepare for and survive these forces of nature. Features include an activity, glossary, list of resources, and index"--Provided by publisher.
    Includes bibliographical references and index.
    ISBN 978-0-7166-9811-1
    1. Epidemics--Juvenile literature. 2. Communicable diseases--Juvenile literature.
  I. World Book, Inc.
  RA653.5.P365 2008
  614.4--dc22

                2007006689

This edition:
ISBN: 978-0-7166-9827-2 (Pandemics)
ISBN: 978-0-7166-9817-3 (set)

Printed in China
1 2 3 4 5 12 11 10 09 08

Editor in Chief: Paul A. Kobasa

Supplementary Publications

    Associate Director: Scott Thomas
    Managing Editor: Barbara A. Mayes

Editors: Jeff De La Rosa, Nicholas Kilzer, Christine Sullivan, Kristina A. Vaicikonis

Researchers: Cheryl Graham, Jacqueline Jasek

Manager, Contracts & Compliance
    (Rights & Permissions): Loranne K. Shields

Graphics and Design

    Associate Director: Sandra M. Dyrlund
    Associate Manager, Design: Brenda B. Tropinski
    Associate Manager, Photography: Tom Evans
    Designer: Matt Carrington

Production

    Director, Manufacturing and Pre-Press: Carma Fazio
    Manager, Manufacturing: Steven Hueppchen
    Manager, Production/Technology: Anne Fritzinger
    Proofreader: Emilie Schrage

Product development: Arcturus Publishing Limited

    Writer: Philip Steele
    Editors: Nicola Barber, Alex Woolf
    Designer: Jane Hawkins
    Illustrator: Stefan Chabluk

Acknowledgments:

The Art Archive: 17 (Biblioteca Nazionale Marciana Venice/ Dagli Orti), 31, 32 (Culver Pictures).

Corbis: 15 (Warrick Page), 16 (Stapleton Collection), 18, 28, 29, 41 (Reuters), 19, 23 (Bettmann), 22 (Historical Picture Archive), 30 (Corbis), 39 (Karen Kasmauski), 40 (Wilson Wen/ epa), 42 (Jens Buettner/ dpa).

Eye of Science/ Photo Researchers: cover/ title page (Digital Vision/ SuperStock).

Science Photo Library: 4 (Mark Clarke), 5 (U.S. National Library of Medicine), 7 (Alfred Pasieka), 8 (Dr. Linda Stannard, UCT), 9 top (NIBSC), 9 bottom (Biophoto Associates), 10 (Grapes/ Michaud), 11 (Richard T. Nowitz), 12 (Dr. Kari Lounatmaa), 13 (Mike Devlin), 14 (Tony Camacho), 20 (Science Source), 24, 35 (Eye of Science), 26 (U.S. Department of Agriculture), 27 (James King-Holmes), 33, 43 (Science Photo Library), 36 (Hank Morgan), 37 (Tony Craddock), 38 (Mauro Fermariello).

TABLE OF CONTENTS

Glossary There is a glossary of terms on pages 45-46. Terms defined in the glossary are in type **that looks like this** on their first appearance on any spread (two facing pages).

Additional resources Books for further reading and recommended Web sites are listed on page 47. Because of the nature of the Internet, some Web site addresses may have changed since publication. The publisher has no responsibility for any such changes or for the content of cited sources.

WHAT IS A PANDEMIC?

A **pandemic** is an outbreak of an **infectious** disease that affects many people over a wide area. Pandemics do not occur very often, but when they do, their effects can be devastating throughout countries, continents, and even the world.

Infectious or noninfectious?

Many different diseases affect human beings, but not all are infectious diseases. Infectious diseases occur when an **organism** gains entry into the body and reproduces itself. Infectious diseases can often be passed from one person to another directly. Contact with a person who has a particular infectious disease can increase another person's risk of developing that disease. Such diseases as chickenpox, influenza (flu), measles, and AIDS are all infectious and can spread through certain kinds of person-to-person contact. Other infectious diseases, such as malaria and cholera, spread indirectly, through water, food, or insect bites.

Illnesses that do not involve invading organisms are said to be **noninfectious.** Contact with someone who has a noninfectious medical condition does not

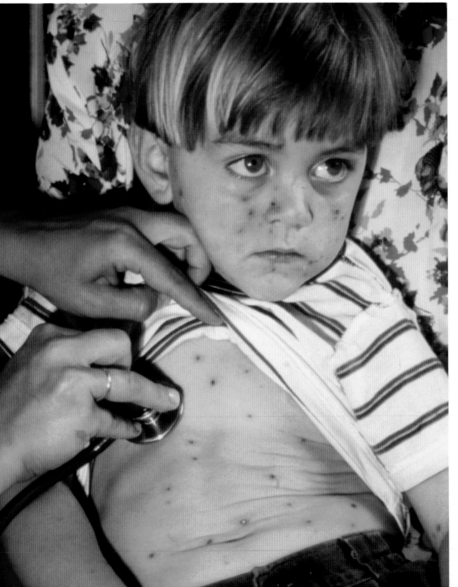

A young boy with chickenpox, an infectious disease that causes itchy spots on the skin.

increase the risk of developing that condition. Cancer, heart disease, and broken bones are all noninfectious medical conditions.

Endemic diseases, epidemics, and pandemics

In any large group of people, some diseases are always present within the group. These are **endemic** diseases. In most countries, the common cold is an endemic disease. There are likely to be some individuals suffering from it at any one time. An **epidemic** is an outbreak of an infectious disease that affects many people at the same time. Epidemics can be local, affecting many people in a small area. They can also be more widespread. A pandemic is similar to an epidemic but covers a much larger area and affects many more people.

An illustration of a medieval street scene depicts a town crier ringing his bell and calling for people to bring out their dead during a plague epidemic.

PANDEMICS IN THE ANCIENT WORLD

Pandemics are not new. Historians know that pandemics occurred thousands of years ago, but historians often lack evidence to identify the disease that caused the pandemic.

■ During the Peloponnesian War (431-404 B.C.), a pandemic began in East Africa, spread through North Africa to Persia, and killed one-third of the population of Greece.

■ The Antonine **Plague** (A.D. 165-180) killed nearly one-third of the population of the Mediterranean region.

■ The Plague of Justinian began around A.D. 540 and killed one-fourth of the population of the eastern Mediterranean. It ravaged the city of Constantinople (now Istanbul) and spread into Western Europe. Not until the 760's did this plague die out.

WHAT CAUSES INFECTIOUS DISEASES?

Infectious diseases are caused by **organisms** so small they cannot be seen with the human eye. They are called **microorganisms,** or microbes. There are four main types: **bacteria, viruses, fungi,** and **parasites.** When they cause disease in people, the various microbes are commonly referred to as **germs.**

Bacteria

Each bacterium is a single **cell.** Most bacteria are less than 1/10,000 inch (1/100 millimeter) long. They have a strong outer layer called the cell wall and an inner layer called the cell **membrane.** Inside the cell is a watery fluid called **cytoplasm.** The **genetic** information—the chemical instructions that determine an organism's traits and that direct growth and reproduction—is stored on a single **chromosome** coiled up in the cytoplasm. **Infectious** diseases that are caused by bacteria include cholera, tuberculosis, and typhoid.

Some bacteria are spherical, some are rod-shaped, and some are spiral-shaped. Some have tiny external threads called flagella that help them to move. Some have an extra outer coat called a capsule.

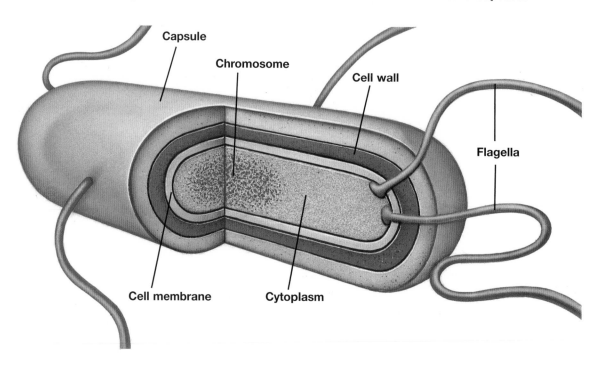

Capsule

Chromosome

Cell wall

Flagella

Cell membrane

Cytoplasm

Viruses

Most viruses are even smaller than bacteria, and they share a basic structure. At the center of a virus is a single coiled strand of genetic material surrounded by a protective **protein** coat. Some virus particles have an extra outer layer called an *envelope.* Infectious diseases caused by viruses include AIDS, chickenpox, influenza, and measles.

Fungi

Molds, mushrooms, and yeasts are all types of fungi. Some fungi are single-celled, but most consist of thousands of fine threads called **hyphae.** These threads form a mesh throughout the material on which they are growing. Some fungi cause such infectious diseases as athlete's foot and thrush, which generally affects the mouth and other moist parts of the body. Fungal diseases do not usually lead to pandemics.

Parasites

Many parasites that cause infectious diseases in human beings are single-celled organisms called **protozoans** that can only be seen under a microscope. Each protozoan has a cell membrane, cytoplasm, and a **nucleus.** Parasites exist in many different shapes. Many of them have tiny hairs called **cilia** or threads called **flagella** to help them move. Infectious diseases caused by parasites include malaria and sleeping sickness.

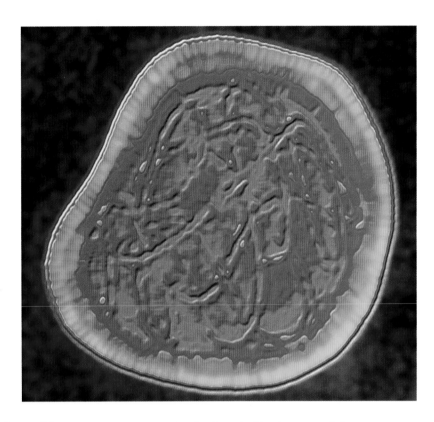

A single rubella virus particle, seen under an electron microscope, has an outer coat (orange-yellow) and a core containing genetic material (red).

GERM THEORY

It was only in the middle of the 1800's that scientists began to understand the link between microorganisms and infectious diseases. Working independently, Louis Pasteur (1822-1895), a French chemist, and Robert Koch (1843-1910), a German physician, both proved that a specific type of microorganism always causes a specific disease. This idea became known as germ theory. The discovery was an important milestone in the study of infectious diseases.

HOW DO MICROORGANISMS MULTIPLY AND SURVIVE?

Infection by a single **microorganism** is unlikely to do much harm. If conditions are not suitable for growth, the microorganism may lie **dormant,** or it may die. But if conditions are right, a single microorganism can multiply rapidly. Within a very short time, a large number of microorganisms may infect the body, causing disease.

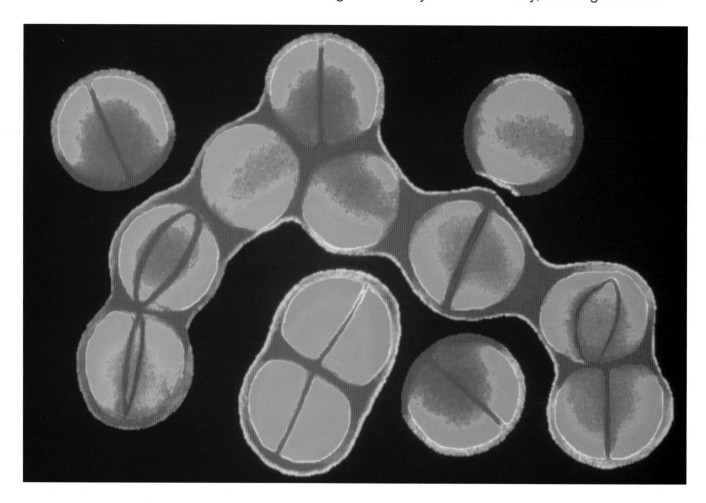

Individual cells of *Staphylococcus aureus* bacteria (light blue) are seen undergoing cell division in an image taken by an electron microscope.

Bacteria

The microbes called **bacteria** multiply by dividing. A single **cell** splits into two new cells. Each of these then grows and splits again to create two more new cells. This process can take place as quickly as once every 20 minutes, and so a large number of bacteria can develop rapidly.

Viruses

Viruses cannot multiply on their own—they must enter a living cell to become active. They take over the cell to produce new virus material and assemble new viruses. This process is called replication. Many new viruses can be produced in this way in as little as an hour.

Fungi

Fungi can multiply in two ways. The simplest is called budding. A tiny area of a fungal cell swells and grows and is eventually pinched off to form a new cell. The type of fungus that causes thrush multiplies by budding. Fungi can also multiply by producing cells called **spores** that can spread and then produce new **hyphae.** The fungus that causes athlete's foot multiplies this way.

Parasites

There are many different types of **parasites,** and they multiply in different ways. Some simply divide to produce new cells; some produce spores; and others have more complicated life cycles.

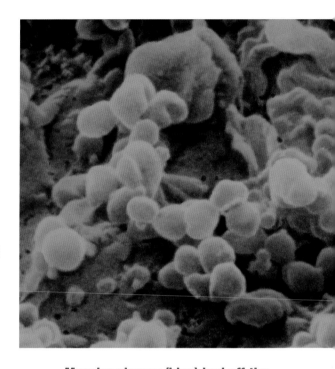

Measles viruses (blue) bud off the surface of an infected cell (green) (above). The fungus that causes athlete's foot (below) appears as a network of thin, branching filaments (hyphae) on flaky skin scales.

MICROORGANISM SURVIVAL

Microorganisms usually need warmth and moisture to multiply. If these conditions are not present, microorganisms need to be able to survive until their **environment** improves. Some bacteria produce spores that can survive very high or very low temperatures for many years. Fungal spores and many virus particles are also able to withstand extreme temperatures and drought conditions. Many parasites can produce eggs or **cysts** that can survive for a long time in soil, water, and other places.

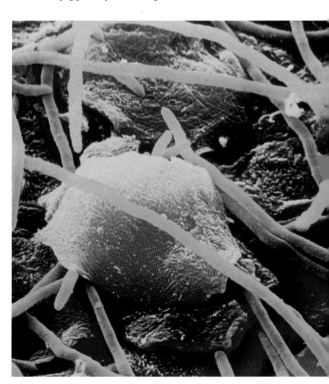

HOW DO INFECTIOUS DISEASES SPREAD?

Infectious diseases can spread in one of several different ways. Some **microorganisms** are passed by direct or indirect contact between an infected person and a healthy person. Other microorganisms are spread through air, water, or food. Some must be carried by an animal.

When we sneeze or cough, microorganisms are propelled into the air and can easily be inhaled by other people, spreading infection.

Infection by contact

Microorganisms can be passed on if an infected person touches a healthy person. Such physical contact may lead to infection in the healthy person, who may then pass the microorganisms on to others in the same way. The virus *Herpes simplex* causes cold sores and is spread by direct contact between people, including through kissing and sharing food or drink. Microorganisms may also be transferred from person to person on such items as kitchen towels or sponges.

Some infections can be spread in body fluids such as blood, **saliva,** and **semen.** Hepatitis B can pass from an infected person through his or her blood, and AIDS can be spread through blood or semen.

Airborne infections

An infection such as the common cold makes people sneeze and cough. The action of sneezing or coughing forces microorganisms out of the body and into the surrounding air. The microorganisms may then be passed on to other people when they breathe the microbes in.

Water-borne infections

Water that is contaminated by microorganisms can spread such serious infections as cholera, which causes severe diarrhea and can be fatal if not treated promptly. Water-borne infections are most common in areas where people do not have access to clean drinking water or where **sanitation** is poor.

Food-borne infections

Microorganisms can grow and multiply in food that is not properly washed, stored, or cooked. When the food is eaten, the microorganisms enter the body and cause various infections that are often referred to as food poisoning. Such infections include listeria and salmonella.

PASSING ON PARASITES

Some infectious diseases rely on other living creatures to spread them. For example, malaria is spread by mosquitoes. The microorganism that causes malaria is a **parasite** called *Plasmodium*. *Plasmodium* multiplies in red blood **cells,** destroying them in the process. If a mosquito bites a person suffering from malaria, the blood it sucks up contains *Plasmodium* cells, which can live inside the mosquito. When the mosquito bites another person, the *Plasmodium* cells are passed on through the mosquito's infected saliva.

The microorganisms that cause malaria, a parasite called *Plasmodium*, are passed from person to person by blood-sucking mosquitoes.

HOW DO MICROORGANISMS AFFECT HUMAN BEINGS?

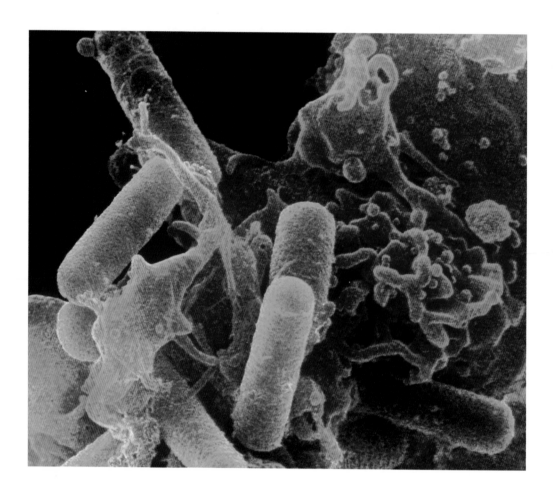

A white blood cell (orange) engulfs bacteria (blue). Once inside the white blood cell, the bacteria will be destroyed.

Microorganisms affect human beings in different ways. Some microbes are helpful, such as the **bacteria** that live in the intestines and help in the process of digestion. However, others can cause infections that may affect a part of the body or even the entire body. Some infections are minor and hardly noticeable, but others can be irritating, painful, or even life threatening.

No entry!

The body's first defense against microorganisms is the skin. The skin is a waterproof layer that acts as a barrier to prevent microorganisms from getting in. Skin produces an oily substance called **sebum** that keeps microorganisms from growing on it. Tiny hairs and sticky **mucus** line the body's airways to trap microorganisms. Tears contain a chemical called *lysozyme* that kills **bacteria. Saliva** helps to keep microorganisms from multiplying inside the mouth.

Inside the body

If microorganisms do enter the body, they can multiply quickly and may cause an infection. Skin may become red and swollen if bacteria infect a wound. Some microorganisms produce chemicals called **toxins** that travel around the body in the blood, causing such symptoms as fever and rashes. Other microorganisms affect specific organs. For example, *Mycobacterium tuberculosis,* which mainly attacks the lungs, causes tuberculosis (TB).

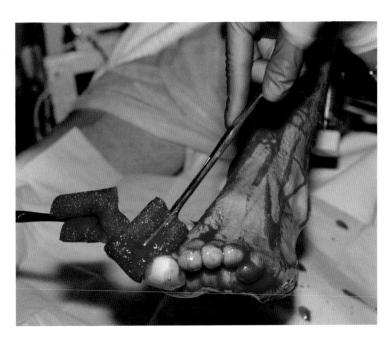

Swabbing a patient's foot with iodine before surgery kills any microorganisms present on the skin and reduces the risk of infection.

Modern medicines and treatments

Many patients with **infectious** diseases can be successfully treated. **Antibiotics** fight bacterial infections by killing bacteria or preventing them from multiplying inside the body. **Antiseptics** help to minimize the risk of infection by killing microorganisms outside the body. **Vaccination** works by introducing tiny amounts of dead or weakened **viruses** or other microorganisms into the body. The process prepares the **immune system** to resist future attacks by those microorganisms. **Antivirals** generally interfere with a virus's ability to duplicate itself.

THE IMMUNE SYSTEM

The immune system, which researchers still do not fully understand, is the body's defense against microorganisms and other disease-causing agents. The system is made up of several parts:

- White blood cells swallow up and kill microorganisms; produce chemicals to target microorganisms; and "remember" microorganisms so that they can mount a swift attack if the microorganisms enter the body in the future.

- Bone marrow produces white blood cells.

- Lymph nodes store white blood cells and trap microorganisms.

- Spleen produces white blood cells and removes some microorganisms from the blood.

- Thymus helps some white blood cells to develop.

As long as conditions remain stable, an **endemic** disease will simply continue to exist within a group. However, a change may occur that makes it easier for the disease to spread, giving rise to a **pandemic.** The change may occur in the **microorganism** itself, in people, or in the **environment.**

HIV, the virus that causes AIDS, is likely to have evolved from viruses that originally infected monkeys and apes in Africa. The virus appears to have been transmitted to people who hunted, butchered, and consumed chimpanzees that were infected with the viruses.

Changes in microorganisms

Every time a microorganism multiplies, its **genetic** information is copied. The process is complicated, and not every copy is perfect. Some copies are slightly different from the original. These genetic changes are called **mutations.**

Many mutations have little or no effect, but others may make the new microorganisms better at infecting people or spreading from person to person. The mutations may improve the microorganisms' ability to survive in harsh conditions, so that they can thrive over a wider geographical area than before or withstand treatments that would normally kill them. Some mutations may even allow a microorganism to infect a different **species.**

Changes in people

Changes in a human population may affect the spread of a disease as well. Trade, tourism, and immigration bring people from different places into contact with each other. When people travel to a new area, they can spread disease to other people who have never been exposed to the disease before.

Environmental changes

Changes in living conditions can also affect infectious diseases. In refugee camps, overcrowding and poor **sanitation** often allow such infections as cholera and typhoid, which causes fever and intestinal problems, to flourish. Human activities such as farming or construction may affect the habitats of disease-carrying insects. Clearing large areas of trees or draining swamps may destroy an insect's habitat, forcing it into areas where it can infect people. Climate change may also alter the spread of **infectious** diseases. An area that was once too cold for a microorganism to survive may become warmer, allowing the microorganism to spread there.

Aid workers spray diesel fumes in a refugee camp to reduce the risk of a cholera outbreak.

ARMIES ON THE MOVE

During a war, large numbers of soldiers may move from one country to another. If they carry with them an infectious disease, they may infect the local people. If the infection is new to the population, the disease may turn into an **epidemic** or even a pandemic. In 1918, the movement of soldiers from the United States to Europe contributed to the spread of influenza.

POPULATION CHANGES AND PANDEMICS

People have always explored the lands around them, taking their goods, skills, and ideas to new places. However, people also carry less welcome things—including diseases.

European exploration of America

When Europeans began to venture across the Atlantic Ocean during the late 1400's and early 1500's, they brought along disease-causing organisms common in the Old World. These included the **microbes** that cause chickenpox, cholera, measles, smallpox, and typhoid. Some historians believe these diseases killed as many as 90 percent of the American Indians in the hardest-hit areas.

Christopher Columbus's first expedition reached the Caribbean Islands in 1492, and other explorers soon followed. In 1519, the Spaniard Hernán Cortés landed in Mexico, and in 1524, another Spaniard, Francisco Pizarro, began to explore South America. As the Europeans traveled through North and South America, they spread Old World diseases in the New World.

An engraving depicts Christopher Columbus and his crew making landfall in the Caribbean and meeting the native inhabitants. The European explorers carried microbes that decimated the American Indian population.

American Indians had never been exposed to these diseases before and so had little **resistance** to them.

The first **epidemic,** which experts think was probably a widespread outbreak of swine fever, struck the Caribbean in 1493. Swine fever is a disease that usually affects pigs but can also cause influenza-like symptoms in people. Other epidemics followed. By 1518, smallpox had killed half the population in the region. Cortés carried smallpox to Mexico, where it killed as many as 150,000 people. **Pandemics** of European diseases ravaged American Indian populations, with typhus killing more than 2 million people by the end of the 1500's and measles killing a similar number during the 1600's.

Diseases from Africa

Another wave of diseases arrived in the early 1500's with the transport of people from West Africa to work as slaves in the Americas. The African slaves were largely unaffected by European diseases because there had been contact between Europe and Africa for thousands of years, allowing Africans to build up resistance. However, Africans themselves carried such tropical diseases as malaria—which causes fever, weakness, seizures, and jaundice—and yellow fever—which affects the liver, kidneys, and heart—that were previously unknown in the Americas. These diseases devastated the native populations of the Caribbean and Central America.

Spanish explorers are greeted by the native Incas of Peru in the 1500's in a period drawing. Europeans were responsible for the spread of many new diseases among the native peoples of South America.

JAPAN'S "AGE OF PLAGUES"

Japan is a country of islands in the western Pacific Ocean. The islands are not linked to the mainland of Asia, and until the A.D. 500's, there was almost no contact between the mainland and island populations. In 552, an outbreak of smallpox occurred, probably following a visit to Japan by Buddhist **missionaries** from the mainland. The outbreak launched an "Age of Plagues" in Japan that lasted for hundreds of years, with more than 100 epidemics and pandemics occurring between 700 and 1050.

THE COURSE OF A PANDEMIC

Pandemics often follow a local outbreak of an **endemic** disease. No matter which disease is involved, the sequence of events that occurs during a pandemic has a similar overall pattern.

Local beginnings

A pandemic begins with an increase in infections in a small geographic area. The disease spreads over a wider area as the number of people with the illness increases. In some cases, a **mutation** may have occurred, making the **microorganism** more dangerous and more easily spread. People traveling on business or vacation may carry the disease to more distant areas.

The spread of a disease

In the past, communication between distant lands was slow. Often, people continued to travel, trade, and socialize before a pandemic was recognized, spreading infections unknowingly. Today, with modern communication technology, people quickly hear about events in the world. Health officials can take action to minimize the spread of a disease outbreak with a minimum of delay after the first cases are reported. There will, however, always be a lag between the time a large number of individuals begin to fall ill and the time a public health response is launched. It takes time for people to see a doctor and receive a diagnosis and for doctors to report the

On a 2003 flight from Manila to Singapore, many passengers wear masks to protect themselves against the spread of Severe Acute Respiratory Syndrome (SARS). Air travel is one way in which an infection can be spread rapidly from one region to another.

outbreak to the authorities. And, in an age of global travel, a person can unknowingly carry a disease to the other side of the world in a matter of hours.

A disease may spread very quickly if it is introduced into an area where people have less **resistance** to the infection. At the peak of a pandemic, the number of people with the illness grows rapidly, and the disease spreads quickly, often claiming many lives.

The pandemic ends

Eventually, the number of people with the illness begins to drop. The remaining population offers a smaller target to the microorganism, and some survivors may have built up some resistance to the disease. Changing environmental conditions may make it more difficult for the microorganism to thrive. Physicians may slow outbreaks through medicines that cure people or by actions that prevent the spread of infection. After a time, the disease becomes confined to those areas in which it was originally endemic.

TYPHUS

Typhus is an **infectious** disease that spreads rapidly in overcrowded conditions, causing aches, a rash, and a high fever that often results in death. It is caused by a group of microorganisms called the rickettsias and is spread from person to person through infected body lice. The first major epidemic of typhus occurred during the religious wars known as the Crusades in the 1400's. Since then, it has reappeared often in times of conflict when armies live in cramped and **unsanitary** conditions.

American soldiers spray mattresses during World War II (1939-1945) to reduce the risk of insect-borne infection. The soldiers wore masks to protect against breathing in the chemical.

THE BLACK DEATH

Outbreaks of an **infectious** disease called the **plague** have occurred again and again throughout human history. One of the worst episodes, known today as the Black Death, was a **pandemic** that raged across Europe during the middle of the 1300's. Historians estimate that by 1400, from 20 to 30 million people had died from the disease—about one-third of the entire population of the continent.

What is the plague?

The plague is caused by a **bacterium** called *Yersinia pestis.* This bacterium usually infects rats and their fleas. The bacteria enter a rat's

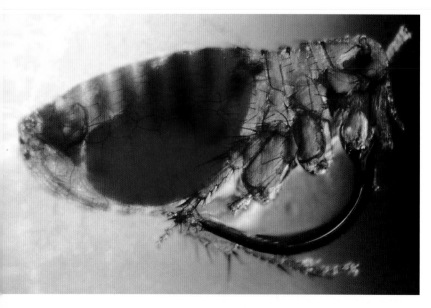

bloodstream when fleas bite, making the rat **host** ill and eventually killing it. When the rat dies, the fleas move to a new host—usually another rat. But the fleas can also live on people. A bite from an infected flea transfers the bacteria to its human victim.

There are three main forms of plague. The most common, bubonic plague, results when a person is bitten by an infected flea. The *Yersinia pestis* bacteria invade the lymph nodes in the legs, groin, neck, and armpits, causing

The black fingerlike mass in this rat flea is caused by infection with *Yersinia pestis,* the microbe that causes plague in humans.

them to swell into large lumps known as buboes. The buboes eventually burst, releasing bacteria into the bloodstream and other parts of the body. The skin blackens and body systems fail. Without medical treatment, about two-thirds of victims die. The buboes gave the disease its grisly name, the "Black Death." Septicemic plague develops when the bacteria multiply in the blood. Pneumonic plague develops if the bacteria invade the lungs. Pneumonic plague is a very dangerous form of the disease because people can spread the bacteria through the air by coughing.

Where did the Black Death come from?

The outbreak of plague known as the Black Death probably began around 1334 in China, where it killed about 5 million people. During the next three years, the plague spread westward along trade routes through Asia, reaching Caffa, a trading post on the Crimean Peninsula by 1346. Caffa, which was under the control of merchants from Genoa in Italy, was under attack by Mongol warriors from Central Asia. Plague hit the Mongol army, and warriors began to die. As they retreated, the Mongols may have catapulted plague-infected bodies into Caffa. The Italian merchants of Caffa fled—but it was too late. Some were already infected with the plague, and many died during the voyage home. Plague traveled on the ships with them and then spread quickly from ports in North Africa and Europe.

EYEWITNESS

Italian author Giovanni Boccaccio (1313?-1375), who lived at the time of the epidemic, described the after effects of the disease:

"Dead bodies filled every corner. Most of them were treated in the same manner by the survivors, who were more concerned to get rid of their rotting bodies than moved by charity towards the dead. ... Such was the multitude of corpses ... that there was not enough consecrated ground to give them burial ... they were forced to dig huge trenches, where they buried the bodies by the hundreds."

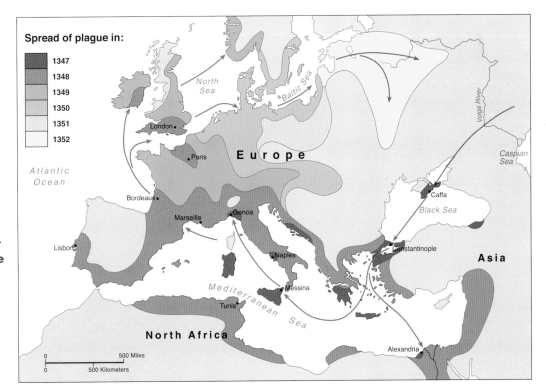

The Black Death— known at that time as the Pestilence or the Great Mortality—spread quickly from Asia into and across Europe in the mid-1300's.

Spread of plague in:

- 1347
- 1348
- 1349
- 1350
- 1351
- 1352

A woodblock print depicts people fleeing to the country during an outbreak of the Black Death. The skeleton coachman suggests that they are carrying the disease, spreading it farther rather than escaping from it!

Life during the Black Death

Because people in towns and cities live close together, **infectious** diseases often spread more easily and rapidly than in the countryside. During the Black Death, many people fled from towns and cities to try to escape infection. However, many of these people were already infected and simply carried the **plague** with them, spreading it farther.

Causes and remedies

At the time of the Black Death, no one knew what caused the disease. Some people thought it was the result of God's anger with human wickedness. Others blamed bad air, which they called "miasma." Although modern medicines can cure plague, there were no effective remedies in the 1300's. A person infected with plague was almost certain to die. Some people tried ringing church bells and firing cannons so that the sound would drive the plague away. In some regions, people lit huge bonfires and burned incense and other perfumes, hoping to clean the air.

Consequences of the Black Death

The Black Death changed Europe forever. So many people died that there were not enough laborers to work the land. The shortage of labor led to demands for higher wages, which were rejected by landowners. The decision led to violent peasant revolts across Europe during the 1300's. Some people began to question the authority of the Roman Catholic Church, which was powerless to explain or prevent the disease. Others blamed the disaster on **minority groups** such as Jews and Roma (often called Gypsies), who suffered **persecution** as a result. People tended to look on the dark side of things following the terrible plague, a view that was reflected in the art and literature of the time. A series of woodcuts called *The Dance of Death* by the German artist Hans Holbein the Younger (1497-1543) depicts death taking people regardless of their wealth or rank.

YERSINIA PESTIS

In 2001, scientists working in Cambridge in the United Kingdom mapped the complete **genetic** sequence, or **genome,** of *Yersinia pestis.* The scientists found evidence indicating that the **bacterium** had originally been a harmless **microorganism** living in the stomach of rats. A series of **mutations** enabled genetic material from other microorganisms to become incorporated into the genome of *Yersinia pestis.* These changes allowed the microorganism to enter the rat's blood, making it much more dangerous for the rat—and for people.

A plague doctor's protective clothing, depicted in a woodblock print from the 1600's, included a hooded robe, glove, goggles, and a bird mask with a beak filled with fresh herbs. The outfit, of course, provided no real protection against infection.

CHOLERA PANDEMICS

Cholera is an **infectious** disease that causes severe diarrhea, resulting in **dehydration.** Most cholera patients today are successfully treated with special solutions that help replace a patient's lost fluids. However, in the 1800's and early 1900's, cholera was feared as a deadly disease for which there was no cure. Scientists now know that cholera is caused by a **bacterium** called *Vibrio cholerae.*

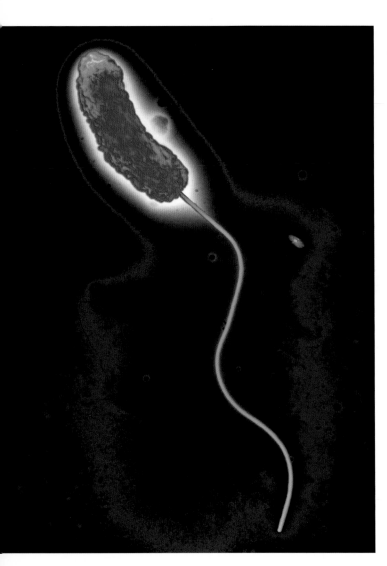

A single *Vibrio cholerae* bacterium, the microbe that causes cholera in humans, has a flagellum, which it uses to help it move.

Understanding cholera

Three scientists in the 1800's improved the understanding of cholera outbreaks. In 1854, John Snow, a British doctor, proved that the disease spread through infected water. Snow plotted all of the cases of cholera in a particular area of London on a map. He noticed that all the cases were tightly centered on a pump from which the people took their drinking water. When he examined a sample of the water under a microscope, he found a bacterium he was unfamiliar with. Snow speculated that the bacterium could be causing the cholera. He removed the pump handle, preventing people from using the well. The cholera cases began to clear up almost immediately.

That same year, Filippo Pacini, an Italian scientist, observed the bacterium and called it *Cholerigenic vibrios.* German doctor Robert Koch joined a team of researchers that traveled to India to study cholera outbreaks. In 1884, Koch managed to grow the bacterium and eventually proved that it was the cause of cholera.

Cholera pandemics

Cholera swept around the world in seven **pandemics** during the 1800's and 1900's, beginning in 1817 and ending about 1970. All of the pandemics began in Asia, but they affected Africa, Europe, and North and South America as well.

Since the seventh pandemic, there have been other cholera outbreaks around the world. However, these outbreaks have been controlled and the spread of the disease restricted using modern medicine. Cholera continues to be a threat in **developing countries** where **sanitation** is poor and clean water unavailable.

THE DANGERS OF CHOLERA

Cholera is spread through infected water. In places where people do not have a supply of clean water, human **feces** containing *Vibrio cholerae* bacteria may **contaminate** the water that the people use for drinking and cooking. Inside the body, the bacteria multiply rapidly in the intestines and produce a **toxin.** The toxin causes the intestines to flush out much more water and salt than normal. The infected person suffers severe diarrhea and becomes dehydrated. Treatment that includes replacement of water and salt can cure cholera. But death can follow within hours of infection without treatment.

Pandemic	When did the pandemic occur?*	Where did the pandemic begin?	Where did the pandemic spread?
1st	1817–1823	India	China, Japan, Iran, Turkey, East Africa, and Mediterranean countries
2nd	1829–1851	India	Russia, Central and Southeast Asia, Europe, North America
3rd	1852–1859	India	Asia, Europe, North and South America, and eventually worldwide
4th	1863–1879	India	Southern Europe, North Africa, and the Middle East
5th	1881–1896	India	East Asia, southern Europe, and South America
6th	1899–1923	India	Asia, the Middle East, and North Africa
7th	1961–1970	Indonesia	Southeast Asia, the Middle East, Russia, China, and some Pacific islands

* End dates are approximate.

STAGES OF A PANDEMIC

After a **pandemic** ends, there is usually a quiet period before another one begins. During this time, governments and other organizations may monitor infection rates and plan strategies to minimize the effects of a future pandemic. According to the World Health Organization (WHO), pandemics emerge through several stages:

1. **Interpandemic** period

During the time between pandemics, the risk of a pandemic outbreak is low. Medical organizations monitor reports of infections around the world. Some infections can pass from animals to people. Infection data, therefore, are collected for both wild and farm animals. Physicians and scientists also watch for any unusual infection that might signal the development of a new type of disease.

Medical researchers study microscope slide samples of chickens infected with the avian influenza virus, type A, strain H5N1.

2. Pandemic alert

A pandemic alert is issued when early warning signs indicate that a pandemic may be about to emerge. Warning signs include identification of a new disease or a new type of an existing disease, changes in the pattern of the spread of a disease, and increased infection rates.

As the alert period progresses, the infection may spread rapidly in a location, causing an **epidemic.** Governments may restrict travel and order **vaccination** programs to prevent an epidemic from developing into a full-scale pandemic. Emergency services may carry out special training to prepare for a pandemic.

3. Pandemic period

The infection may spread despite all efforts to limit the disease during the second stage, developing into a pandemic.

Boxes containing syringes filled with the influenza vaccine Enzira in a storage refrigerator. The vaccine protected against three strains (types) of the flu virus that health officials expected would be the most common in 2006 and 2007.

WORLD HEALTH ORGANIZATION (WHO)

The World Health Organization is a United Nations agency that was established in 1948. Its headquarters are in Geneva, Switzerland. WHO plays a major part in detecting and monitoring **infectious** diseases. The organization pays for and carries out medical research, trains medical workers, and provides emergency aid wherever it is needed. WHO also offers advice to governments about how they can prevent the outbreak of diseases and improve the health of their people.

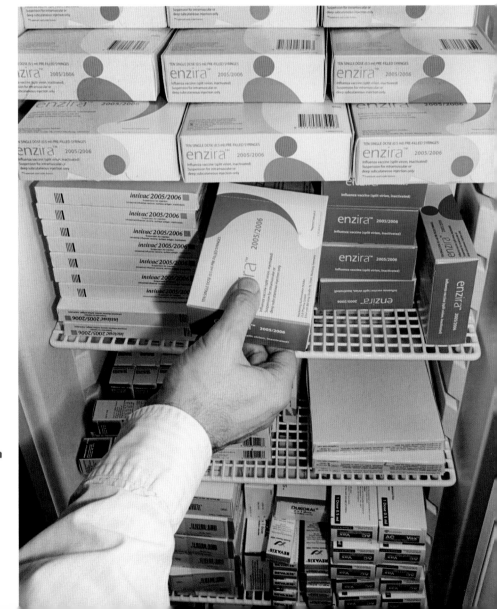

PANDEMIC!

Nearly everyone in the world is affected in some way when a **pandemic** develops. People can be affected directly—by catching the infection—or indirectly—by the social and economic consequences of the pandemic.

Restrictions

If a pandemic were to begin, the movement of people would likely be restricted to minimize the spread of infection. The restrictions may include travel to and from countries hit by the pandemic. People traveling from infected areas would have to spend time in **quarantine,** where they would be isolated from other people until it was clear that they do not have the disease. Some health experts have recommended that in extreme circumstances, people be forcibly quarantined to protect the rest of the population. Other restrictions might include closing such public places as theaters or libraries within the affected area, reducing transportation services, and limiting nonessential travel.

Health services

Most hospitals are busy places even in normal times. In the event of a pandemic, many doctors and nurses would be reassigned from

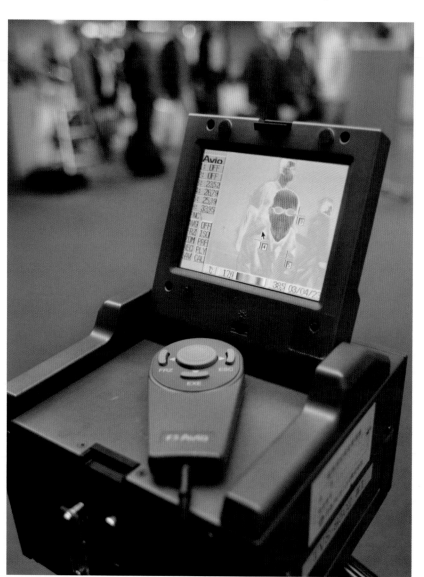

A thermal video system monitors the temperature of passengers arriving at New Tokyo International airport in Japan in 2003. The monitoring was part of an effort to detect cases of Severe Acute Respiratory Syndrome (SARS).

their regular duties to help with the large numbers of infected people. Medical staff, including orderlies and assistants, would also be taken from their usual duties to help treat victims of the pandemic.

Communication, work, and education

During a pandemic, governments would make public announcements explaining what people should do to protect themselves and describing any new restrictions or regulations. To slow the spread of the disease, schools and day care centers might close. Offices, stores, and factories would also close as people were advised to avoid public places. Many services, including banking and postal services, would be disrupted.

Supplies

Transportation restrictions and illness among workers during a pandemic would likely disrupt the delivery of goods and fuel in many areas. Energy supplies, such as gasoline, would likely be limited. In a severe pandemic, **rationing** of essential items may be necessary.

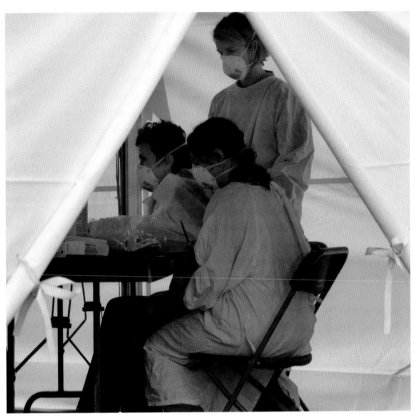

Medical staff work in a tent set up outside St. Vincent Hospital in Vancouver, Canada, during the SARS outbreak in 2003. Such facilities helped to relieve overcrowded emergency rooms.

PLANNING FOR A PANDEMIC

In a televised interview in 2005, Australian Health Minister Tony Abbott discusses Australia's plans for a possible avian influenza pandemic:

"One of the elements of our pandemic preparedness is our quarantine stockpiles, so we can keep the people who have just arrived on a jumbo jet for instance, [from] a country that has confirmed bird flu and has people who are possibly symptomatic on the plane, we can keep all of them in quarantine for the seven to ten days it would take until the disease had passed. ... We have plans for an escalating health response, including mobile teams, home quarantine, home treatment, so that only the very serious cases have to go to public hospitals. ..."

THE INFLUENZA PANDEMIC, 1918-1919

For many people, an outbreak of influenza, or flu, is just a normal part of winter. But the influenza outbreak of 1918-1919 was one of the worst **pandemics** humanity has ever suffered. Experts estimate that worldwide about 25 million people died during the 18 months of the pandemic.

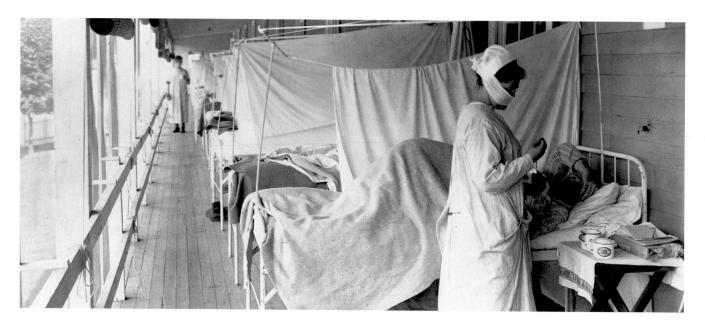

Overcrowding during the great influenza pandemic causes additional wards to be set up on porches at an Army hospital in Washington, D.C., in 1918.

What caused the pandemic?

Influenza is caused by a virus. There are three main types of the influenza virus, known as type A, type B, and type C. Each has many variations, or **subtypes.** In people, most influenza is caused by type A or B viruses.

An influenza virus is often named for the place where it initially strikes. In the 1918–1919 pandemic, the virus became known as the "Spanish flu" because the Spanish government—unlike the governments of other countries—made no secret of how severely the disease had affected Spain. Many researchers believe the pandemic may have actually begun in the United States.

In 2005, researchers determined the complete **genome** of the 1918 virus. Some scientists think the genome indicates that the virus came from a type of influenza virus that normally affects only birds.

Pandemic

Early in the morning of March 11, 1918, a soldier went to the camp hospital at Fort Riley, Kansas. He did not seem to be seriously ill, but he had a headache, fever, and sore throat. He was quickly joined by another soldier, and then another, until by lunchtime there were more than 100 cases in the hospital. Other soldiers had carried the virus with them when they traveled to Europe to fight in World War I (1914-1918). But at this stage, the infection did not seem particularly serious.

In July 1918, influenza took hold in Poland. By August, people noticed that the infection was becoming more deadly. It seemed that **pneumonia** often developed after a person became infected, and many patients died within 48 hours of the appearance of influenza symptoms. This infection also spread very rapidly from person to person. By the autumn of 1918, the influenza pandemic had spread around the world, following the patterns of trade routes and shipping lines.

U.S. soldiers, departing for France in 1918, march through the streets of Seattle, Washington, wearing masks intended to provide protection from influenza infection.

Country	Estimated number of influenza deaths
Australia	more than 14,000
France	about 240,000
India	about 18,500,000
United Kingdom	more than 230,000
United States	more than 600,000
Worldwide	about 25,000,000

THE BLUE DEATH

By September 1918, the flu had traveled back across the Atlantic to the United States in its much more dangerous form. Some people began to call the illness the "Blue Death," because in its later stages, victims' skin turned blue or purple from a lack of oxygen. Philadelphia, Pennsylvania, was one of the cities hardest hit by the influenza. The city had not only great numbers of workers in the factories of the war industry but also a large naval base and shipyard. In a single day at the height of the pandemic, Philadelphia's death toll reached 1,700. City workers patrolled the streets with horse-drawn carts, calling to residents to bring out their dead. The drivers delivered the wagonloads of bodies to a potter's field for burial in mass graves.

Treating the sick

With so many people suffering and dying from influenza, governments were forced to take drastic action. There were not enough hospitals or medical staff to treat the huge numbers of people who were ill. Volunteers helped with nursing care, and many medical students were given duties. In the United States and other countries, temporary hospitals were set up in such places as school halls, gymnasiums, and community centers.

A conductor refuses to allow a man onto a streetcar in Seattle, Washington, because he was not wearing a protective face mask during the influenza pandemic.

Controlling the spread

Governments around the world did many things to combat the spread of the disease. One effective method was the use of **quarantine** to reduce contact between people. Many theaters, churches, schools, factories, and stores were ordered to close. Posters advised people on the precautions they should take to avoid catching or spreading influenza. In the United States, people were given face masks to wear in public places to prevent the spread of the virus. One slogan of the day urged people to "Obey the laws and wear the gauze; protect your jaws from septic paws." Some bus and train companies refused to carry passengers who were not wearing masks. In Japan, travel in and out of the country was severely limited.

Anti-influenza remedies?

People were so frightened of the flu that they were ready to try almost anything to avoid it. Some companies sold products they said were effective at preventing infection. Others sold such products as herbal drinks that they claimed would strengthen the **immune system** and help people fight off the flu. Such products were ineffective.

Burying the dead

The death rate from the 1918-1919 flu pandemic was extraordinarily high, because the virus involved was much deadlier than those responsible for other flu pandemics. In the first months of the pandemic, 25 million people died, compared with 25 million deaths from AIDS in the first five years of that **epidemic.** One man described his childhood memories of the flu pandemic in the United States: "The first time that I was aware that something was amiss in our normal living was when my father told me, 'Son, most of the employees are sick. We don't have anyone left to run the store. Everyone is home sick, or in the hospital sick.' And within a week or ten days my father told me that this saleslady had passed away and another one had passed away. So, as I recall, out of the eight or ten employees, four of them passed away and the passing away came about so quickly."

Posters, which were displayed in U.S. theaters during 1918, provided information about the influenza pandemic.

AGE AND INFLUENZA

The very young, who have not been previously exposed and developed **resistance** to the **virus,** and the elderly, who may be too frail to overcome the infection, are most at risk in influenza outbreaks. However, in the 1918–1919 pandemic, about half of those who died were from 30 to 40 years old. Scientists are still trying to understand why the virus hit this group unusually hard.

INFLUENZA

FREQUENTLY COMPLICATED WITH

PNEUMONIA

IS PREVALENT AT THIS TIME THROUGHOUT AMERICA.

THIS THEATRE IS CO-OPERATING WITH THE DEPARTMENT OF HEALTH.

YOU MUST DO THE SAME

IF YOU HAVE A COLD AND ARE COUGHING AND SNEEZING. DO NOT ENTER THIS THEATRE

GO HOME AND GO TO BED UNTIL YOU ARE WELL

Coughing, Sneezing or Spitting Will Not Be Permitted In The Theatre. In case you must cough or Sneeze. do so in your own handkerchief. and if the Coughing or Sneezing Persists Leave The Theatre At Once.

This Theatre has agreed to co-operate with the Department Of Health in disseminating the truth about Influenza. and thus serve a great educational purpose.

HELP US TO KEEP CHICAGO THE HEALTHIEST CITY IN THE WORLD

JOHN DILL ROBERTSON

COMMISSIONER OF HEALTH

HIV AND AIDS

AIDS (acquired immunodeficiency syndrome) is the final stage of infection with the human immunodeficiency virus (HIV). Cases of AIDS were first identified in 1981 in the United States, but researchers have detected HIV in a specimen collected in 1959 in central Africa. Since the 1980's, the disease has spread rapidly, reaching **epidemic** levels in some parts of the world. Medical experts believe that an AIDS **pandemic** is taking place worldwide. According to the World Health Organization, more than 25 million people have died of AIDS.

The spread of the AIDS pandemic around the world, and the areas that are most severely affected.

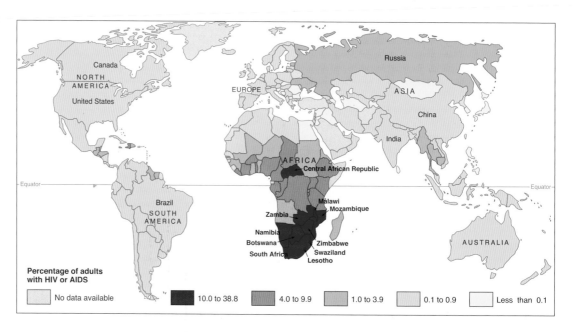

Percentage of adults with HIV or AIDS

No data available | 10.0 to 38.8 | 4.0 to 9.9 | 1.0 to 3.9 | 0.1 to 0.9 | Less than 0.1

What causes AIDS?

AIDS is caused by a virus that attacks the body's **immune system.** Like all viruses, HIV cannot reproduce itself. It enters the white blood **cells** of its **host** and produces new virus particles, killing the white blood cells in the process. The body makes new white blood cells, but the virus destroys them as fast as the body can produce them, and so their numbers decrease. The immune system cannot function properly without a sufficient number of white blood cells.

The spread of HIV

HIV is passed from one person to another through such body fluids as blood and **semen.** It is most commonly spread by unprotected sexual contact with an infected person or by drug addicts who share contaminated needles. HIV can also be spread from a mother to her baby during pregnancy or through her breast milk. **Developed countries** now take precautions to ensure that blood and other products for medical use are free of HIV. But in other parts of the world, infected blood— given in transfusions, for example—is still a significant source of infection.

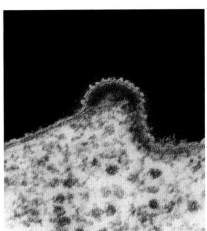
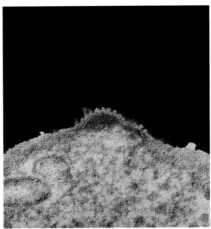
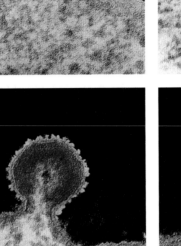
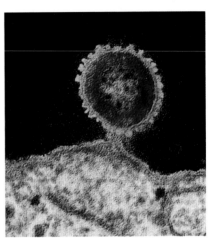

An HIV particle (red/green) emerges from a white blood cell (beige/white). The sequence shows the HIV particle beginning to break through the cell surface (top left) through to its separation from the white blood cell (bottom right).

The impact of HIV and AIDS

Medical experts estimate that more than 35 million people worldwide have HIV and that more than one-third of people with HIV live in Africa south of the Sahara. AIDS has devastated whole communities in this region, leaving millions of children without parents. A generation of African grandmothers is raising 12 million AIDS orphans. The disease has drastically reduced the number of able workers, leaving few survivors in some areas to plant crops and tend animals.

WHERE DID AIDS BEGIN?

Scientists are still trying to find out where HIV came from. One theory, supported by **genetic** evidence, is that HIV developed from a virus that infected monkeys and apes in Africa. It may have been passed to people who hunted and ate the meat of the infected monkeys. **Mutations** in the virus may then have enabled it to pass from person to person.

Diagnosis

Physicians diagnose infection with HIV from a blood sample. The body's **immune system** produces **proteins** called **antibodies** when it detects a virus. A unique antibody is produced for each type of **virus.** If a person has been infected with HIV, antibodies are detected in the blood. The person is then said to be "HIV positive."

Physicians diagnose AIDS when the number of white blood **cells** in an HIV-positive person drops below a certain level. The disease may also be diagnosed when a person begins to suffer from illnesses that often occur when the immune system fails.

Treatment

There is no **vaccine** that prevents HIV infection and no known cure. Combinations of **antiviral** drugs can block the action of HIV. However, these drugs often cause severe side effects. They are also expensive, and so most people in **developing countries** are unable to afford them.

Scientists carry out DNA sequencing, an important part of the research to develop an AIDS vaccine.

Prevention

There are several ways to reduce the spread of HIV:

- Individuals can avoid unprotected sexual contact with a person infected with the virus.
- Drug abuse prevention clinics can ensure that drug addicts have access to **sterile** needles and do not share injecting equipment.
- Doctors, nurses, and other medical professionals can use protective clothing during medical procedures.
- Laboratories can screen blood and blood products for medical use.
- Infected mothers can undergo drug treatment during pregnancy and delivery to reduce their chances of passing HIV to their babies.

These measures can be effective only if people know about them, understand them, and follow them.

HIV, AIDS, AND DISCRIMINATION

Living with HIV and AIDS can be difficult, not just because of the illness itself, but also because of the attitude of other people. **Discrimination** has caused some HIV-positive people to lose their jobs and homes. Some schools are unwilling to accept children with AIDS. Such attitudes can make people reluctant to get tested for HIV. However, treatment of the illness cannot begin if someone does not know that he or she has HIV. Such a person will not realize that there is a need to take precautions to avoid passing the virus to others.

A sign outside a hospital in a border town between India and Bhutan warns of the dangers of AIDS.

PREVENTING A PANDEMIC

Government leaders, scientists, medical workers, and individuals can all take measures to reduce the likelihood of a **pandemic.** Poor living conditions often put people at risk for infection. In many **developing countries,** poor **sanitation** and lack of clean water lead to outbreaks of cholera and other water-borne infections. Disease outbreaks can be reduced or prevented with improved housing, access to clean water supplies, and adequate sanitation.

Individuals can help

If every person remembered to do a few simple things, the spread of **infectious** diseases could be limited. Public health experts recommend:

- Covering the mouth and nose with a handkerchief when coughing or sneezing or coughing and sneezing into the elbow.
- Refraining from spitting in public.
- Washing hands with soap and water after using the toilet.
- Following food storage, preparation, and cooking instructions carefully.
- Avoiding unprotected sexual contact.

Good personal hygiene can help to reduce infections.

Government leaders can help ensure that people are aware of these measures, but it is each individual's responsibility to follow the advice.

Medical measures

Physicians and other medical workers help prevent pandemics by reporting infectious diseases. They notice unusual illnesses and increased numbers of a known infection and inform national and international organizations. Medical workers constantly monitor worldwide health.

Scientists conduct research to develop new medicines to combat infections. They also develop new **vaccines** to provide immunity against particular diseases. Vaccination programs to combat a variety of common infectious diseases help ensure that a large proportion of the population is protected.

Red Cross workers making door-to-door announcements that a measles vaccine is available during an immunization drive in Kenya in 2003.

HOW DO VACCINES WORK?

A vaccine contains dead or weakened **microorganisms.** When the vaccine is injected into the body, the **immune system** responds by attacking and destroying the microbes. During this process, the immune system develops memory **cells** that recognize a live form of the microorganism if it enters the body again. The cells respond rapidly, alerting the rest of the immune system, and the microorganisms are destroyed before an infection can take hold. Some vaccines provide lifetime protection, but others need an additional injection called a booster after a few years.

SARS

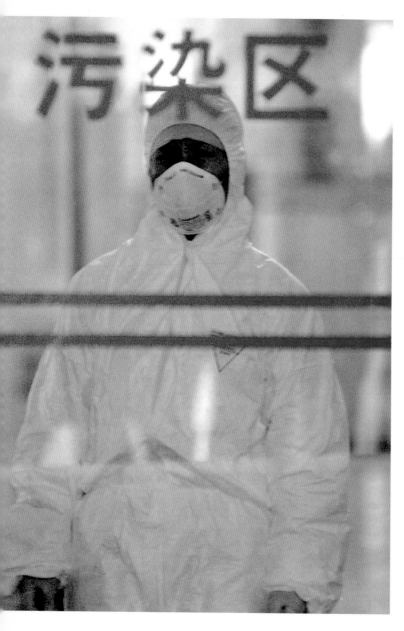

In November 2002, government officials in China reported an outbreak of an **infectious** disease that affected the lungs. Patients developed a fever, cough, and breathing difficulties. About 1 in 10 infected people died. At first, physicians thought they were dealing with a form of influenza or pneumonia. However, by 2003, it had become clear that the illness was a completely new disease. The condition came to be called severe acute respiratory syndrome (SARS).

The spread of SARS

The disease was carried to Hong Kong by an infected physician who had worked on some of the first cases of SARS in China. From there, it spread rapidly through East Asia. Cases were soon reported in North America and later in Europe. The World Health Organization officially classified SARS as a disease threat in March 2003. The number of cases grew rapidly. By the end of May 2003, more than 8,000 had been reported.

A medical worker wearing full protective gear stands inside an isolated area for SARS patients at a hospital in China, in 2004.

Treating SARS

Medical workers were particularly at risk from SARS, because their work brought them into direct contact with infected patients. A method called *barrier nursing* was used to reduce risk. The medical staff was careful never to touch a patient directly, but rather through a **sterile** barrier that was maintained between them.

Antibiotics were found to be of no help in treating SARS, because the illness was caused by a virus. Antiviral drugs that were available also proved ineffective. Doctors were able to do little more than provide breathing assistance and nursing care to victims.

Limiting the spread

Governments worldwide enacted measures to limit the spread of SARS. In some areas, such public buildings as schools and theaters were closed. Many people wore face masks and surgical gloves when they went out in public to avoid infection. Travel was restricted—especially in Asia—and quarantine regulations were enforced.

School students wore masks in some schools in Indonesia in 2003, to protect them from the spread of SARS.

The end of SARS

The number of new cases of SARS fell after May 2003. Two years later, the World Health Organization declared that the spread of SARS had officially been stopped. There were no new cases reported anywhere in the world. Although the threat from SARS was over for the time being, scientists continued to work on developing a vaccine that would offer protection against a future outbreak of SARS.

WHAT CAUSED SARS?

Scientists investigating the outbreak of SARS identified a type of virus known as a *coronavirus*. The name coronavirus—from the Latin word *corona*, which means *crown*—comes from the crown-like ring of bumps on the surface of each virus particle. Other coronaviruses cause pneumonia and the common cold in people as well as a variety of diseases in animals. Scientists found that the SARS coronavirus may have developed from a virus that normally infects bats.

AVIAN INFLUENZA

Avian influenza, also known as bird flu, is an **infectious** disease that normally affects birds. Occasionally, it can also be passed on to people. The first cases of avian influenza in human beings appeared in 1997. Since then, there have been several outbreaks reported, mainly in China and other countries in Asia. An outbreak in 2003 caused great alarm, because bird flu seemed to be on the brink of developing into a **pandemic.**

What causes avian influenza?

Avian influenza, which was first identified in 1961 in South Africa, is caused by the type A influenza **virus.** Although the virus is present in wild birds, it does not usually affect them. The virus can pass easily from wild birds to such domesticated birds as chickens, ducks, and turkeys. After a domestic flock is infected, the virus passes rapidly from bird to bird, killing many. Wild birds

German soldiers wearing protective clothing retrieve a dead swan after the dangerous H5N1 virus, avian flu, was confirmed in more than 100 wild birds on the German island of Rügen in 2006.

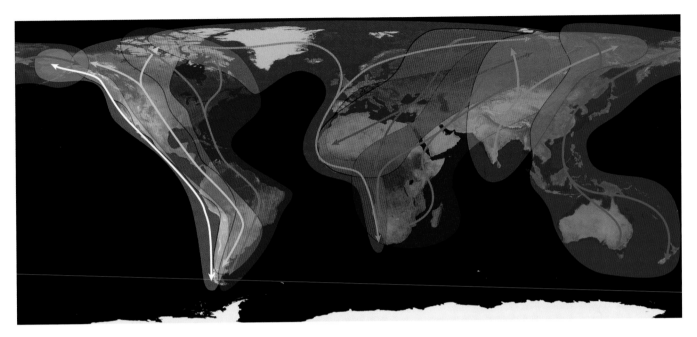

spread the virus to other parts of the world as they migrate. Scientists monitor the migration patterns of birds and report outbreaks of infection to identify areas that might be at risk.

Public health officials suggest that avian flu is spread along bird migratory routes, shown here on a satellite map of the world.

From birds to people?

Occasionally, people have been infected with avian influenza. The infections in human beings were caused by a **subtype** of the virus called H5N1. Most people who were infected had direct and close contact with infected birds or **contaminated** surfaces.

Person to person

The H5N1 virus does not pass easily from person to person. So, bird flu is unlikely to develop into an **epidemic** or pandemic among people. However, like all viruses, H5N1 is constantly changing. Scientists worry that a **mutation** of H5N1 may increase the microbe's ability to pass from person to person, making avian influenza very dangerous for human beings.

PANDEMIC ALERT!

In 2005, H5N1 infections in people were identified in several Asian countries, including Cambodia, China, Thailand, and Vietnam. By early 2006, such infections had also been reported in Egypt, Iraq, and Turkey. Public health authorities quickly took action to control the spread of infection. They ordered the destruction of all birds on poultry farms where the infection was found, restricted the transport of domestic birds, and monitored the migration of wild birds. Such actions controlled the outbreak, and the danger of a human pandemic receded. However, health officials continue to monitor these areas for signs of infection.

ACTIVITY

CAN YOU PREVENT MICROORGANISMS FROM GROWING?

Equipment

- 2-cup (½-liter) pitcher or bowl
- Three clean, transparent containers that hold about a cup (¼ liter) each
- Measuring spoons and cups
- Sugar
- Very hot water (not quite boiling—**ask an adult to help with the hot water!**)
- Warm water
- Dried yeast
- Ice water
- Three regular spoons

Instructions

1. Pour ⅔ cup (160 milliliters) warm water into a pitcher or bowl.

2. Add two teaspoonfuls of sugar and stir until it dissolves.

3. Add the dried yeast and stir.

4. Divide the yeast liquid equally between the three containers.

5. Add ⅓ cup (80 milliliters) of very hot water to the first container, ⅓ cup (80 milliliters) of warm water to the second, and ⅓ cup (80 milliliters) of ice water to the third. Label each container.

6. Stir well, using a different spoon for each.

7. Leave the first container in a hot place, the second container in a warm place, and the third in a refrigerator. Observe after half an hour and then after another half-hour.

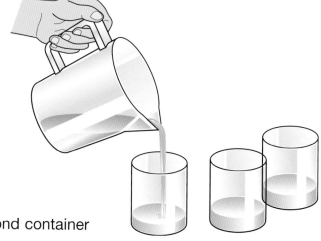

You should find that the container with warm water has a layer of froth. The froth is made by the yeast cells as they grow and divide. It is proof that the cells are alive. If there is no froth, the yeast cells are not growing. Is there froth in the container of hot water or in the one with ice water? What does this tell you about the presence of microorganisms in these containers?

antibiotic A substance produced by living things, such as fungi, that can be used to destroy harmful bacteria.

antibody A substance made by human beings and animals to fight off foreign substances that invade the body, such as viruses and bacteria.

antiseptic A type of chemical that kills microorganisms outside the body.

antiviral A medicine used to combat viral infections.

bacterium (plural, bacteria) A living thing made up of a single cell. Some bacteria cause disease, while others are helpful to human beings.

cell The basic unit of all living matter. All living things are made of cells.

chromosome A strand of genetic material.

cilia (singular, cilium) Tiny hairs or threads.

contaminate To make dirty or harmful.

cyst A dormant stage in the life cycle of some microorganisms.

cytoplasm The fluid inside a cell.

dehydration A condition caused by the excessive loss of fluids from the body.

developed country Any of the richer countries of the world, where living standards are generally high.

developing country Any of the poorer countries of the world, where living standards are generally low.

discrimination A bias against someone for reasons such as gender, religion, or disability.

dormant Describes something that is alive but not active.

endemic Diseases that occur regularly among a particular group or in a particular area.

environment Everything that is outside a living being forms that being's environment.

epidemic An outbreak of disease above normal endemic levels.

feces Solid waste matter from a human or animal body.

flagellum (plural, flagella) A whiplike thread.

fungus (plural, fungi) A type of microorganism that reproduces by spores.

genetic Describes the passing on of characteristics of living organisms from one generation to the next.

genome The genetic code by which characteristics are passed from one generation to the next in a living organism.

germ A microorganism that causes a disease.

host An organism on which a parasite lives and from which the parasite gets its food.

hypha (plural, hyphae) The threadlike mesh formed by some fungi.

immune system The body's defense mechanism against disease.

infectious Describes a disease that is able to pass from person to person.

interpandemic The period between pandemics.

membrane A thin layer.

microorganism (microbe) A living thing too small to be seen except with a microscope.

minority group A group of people who are different in some ways from the main groups in a society.

missionary a person sent by a religious group to convert others to his or her faith.

mucus A thick, slimy fluid.

mutation A change in the genetic information in an organism's cells.

noninfectious Describes a disease that is unable to pass from person to person.

nucleus The part of a cell that controls all the processes of the cell.

organism An individual plant or animal.

pandemic An outbreak of an infectious disease that affects many people over a wide area.

parasite An organism that lives and feeds off another organism (the host).

persecution Describes bad treatment of a person, often because of his or her beliefs.

plague A infectious disease caused by a bacterium.

pneumonia A disease in which the lung or lungs are inflamed.

protein Complex organic compounds that are essential to the functioning as well as the structure of all plant and animal life.

protozoan A type of one-celled organism that may cause disease in human beings.

quarantine The isolation of people from others in order to restrict the spread of infection.

ration To restrict the amount of something.

resistance The ability to withstand something.

saliva A liquid produced in the mouth.

sanitation Drainage, sewage, and other controls that are necessary for good hygiene.

sebum An oily substance produced by the skin.

semen A sperm-carrying liquid produced by males.

species A group of organisms that share the same basic characteristics and can interbreed.

spore A seedlike stage in the life cycle of some organisms.

sterile Free from all microorganisms.

subtype A small group within a larger group.

toxin A poison produced by a living organism.

unsanitary Something that is not clean and hygienic.

vaccination The practice of inoculating a person with a vaccine to prevent or lessen the effects of a disease.

vaccine Any preparation, especially one of bacteria or viruses of a particular disease, used to inoculate a person in order to prevent or lessen the effects of that disease.

virus A tiny organism that can reproduce or grow only by entering the cell of another living thing. Viruses cause many serious diseases.

BOOKS

An American Plague: The True and Terrifying Story of the Yellow Fever Epidemic of 1793,
    by Jim Murphy, Clarion Books, 2003.

Deadly Invaders: Virus Outbreaks Around the World, from Marburg Fever to Avian Flu,
    by Denise Grady, Kingfisher, 2006.

Epidemics and Plagues, by Richard Walker, Kingfisher, 2006.

Eyewitness: Epidemic, by Brian Ward, Dorling Kindersley, 2000.

Flu: The Story of the Great Influenza Pandemic, by Gina Kolata, Touchstone, 2001.

The Ghost Map, by Steven Johnson, Riverhead Hardcover, 2006.

WEB SITES

http://virus.stanford.edu/uda/

http://www.amnh.org/nationalcenter/infection

http://www.kidshealth.org/kid/talk/qa/germs.html

http://www.pandemicflu.gov/general

http://www.themiddleages.net/plague.html

http://www.who.int/csr/don/en

INDEX